Painting

Deri Robins

QED Publishing

First published in the UK in 2004 by
QED Publishing
A division of Quarto Publishing plc
The Fitzpatrick Building
188–194 York Way, London N7 9QP

A Catalogue record for this book is available
from the British Library.

ISBN 1 84538 046 0

Written by Deri Robins
Designed by Wladek Szechter/
Jacqueline Palmer
Edited by Sian Morgan/Matthew Harvey
Artwork by Melanie Grimshaw
Photographer Michael Wicks
With thanks to Nicola

Creative Director Louise Morley
Editorial Manager Jean Coppendale

Picture credits

The Art Archive /18 top Eileen Tweedy, Tate
Gallery, London/
Corbis /29 bottom Roger De La Harpe, Gallo
Images

Printed and bound in China

The words in **bold** are
explained in the Glossary
on page 30.

Contents

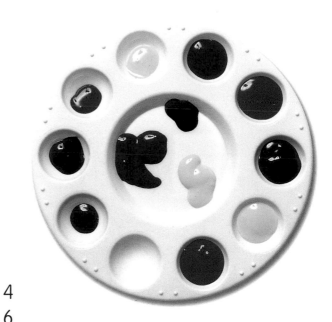

Tools and paints

You only need a few brushes and a simple paint set to get started – but it's a good idea to build up a collection of some of the equipment below if you want to experiment with different effects.

Pencils

Soft-lead pencils (such as 9B) are useful for sketching the outlines of your pictures before adding paint. Use coloured pencils to add detail.

Brushes

Different brushes give different results. You need a fine, pointed one for detail, a middle thickness one and a really thick one for large areas. Nylon bristles are best for thin paint, and hogs' hair brushes are better for thick paint. Use an old toothbrush for spattering (see pages 28–29), and sponges and rags for dabbing (see pages 12–13).

pencils

Palettes and pots

You can buy artists' **palettes** for mixing colours – but an old plastic tray, an old plate or piece of smooth wood are just as good. Use jam jars full of water to clean your brushes.

Bits and pieces

Use newspaper to protect your work surface and a roll of kitchen towel to dry your brushes. Collect ideas in a notebook or **sketchbook** when you are out. Paste things that inspire you, such as coloured paper, leaves and magazine cuttings into your books.

brushes

palette

watercolours

acrylic paints

ink

gouache paints

Paint

Poster paints are ideal for big, bold paintings, or to mix with other things to create texture (see pages 22–23). Use them straight from the container or thin them down with water.

Watercolours are delicate colours that make great landscapes. They come in tubes or blocks, are easy to carry and handy for colour sketches.

Gouache paints produce strong, vibrant colours that are good to use on coloured papers.

Paper

It's important to use good paper. Smooth cartridge paper is best. The paint doesn't sink into the surface and become dull. Thick paint on rough sugar paper can be interesting. Watercolour paper is thick, so that it doesn't wrinkle when it gets wet.

art paper

poster paints

5

Colour mixing

Mixing colours is one of the most important things you will need to do as a painter. Take time to read these pages, and try out lots of colour experiments of your own.

Make it up

Nearly every colour you can think of is made up from just three **primary** colours: red, blue and yellow. Here's how to mix paints to get all the colours you need.

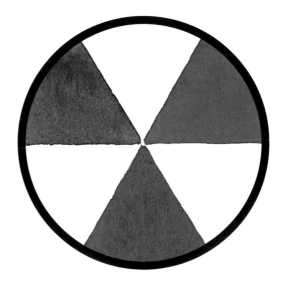

Primary colours

Red, yellow and blue are called the primary colours because you cannot make them from any other colours.

Secondary colours

Mix any two primary colours together and you get a **secondary** colour. They are orange, green and purple.

Colour wheel

The inner rim of the wheel shows what happens when you mix primary colours: red and yellow make orange; red and blue make purple; and yellow and blue make green.

The outer rim shows what happens when you mix secondary colours together. You get six more colours.

Make your own colour wheel and try different colour combinations.

TIP

Make your own colour charts, like the ones at DIY stores, then personalize them. Draw small rectangles on a sheet of paper. Fill each with a different **shade** – choose a range of blues or a range of pinks, for example. Give them a name, such as 'princess pink', or 'sea-haze green'. Remember to make a note of the colours you used to mix them – and how much of each colour you used.

Complementary colours

Colours that are opposite each other on the colour wheel are called **complementary** colours. Put them together and they can make paintings exciting and make the colours seem deeper.

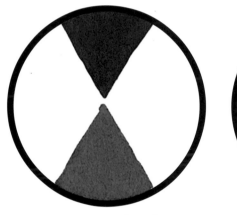

green and red

yellow and violet

blue and orange

Making colours darker

Don't just add black to make a darker colour: often this just makes it look dull and boring. Instead, add a tiny bit of a different, darker colour. Experiment on scrap paper until you get a shade that you like.

Lighten up

Add more water to watercolour paint for lighter **shades**. With poster or powder paint, just add a little white paint at a time, until you get the shade you want.

Warm and cool

Colours can be described as 'cool' (such as green and blue) or 'warm' (orange, yellow and red). You can use these colours to create cool, calm paintings or hot, exciting ones.

Greys and browns

Black and white is only one way to make grey. You can get more interesting shades of grey by mixing different amounts of the three primary colours together or two complementary colours.

There are many different shades of brown, too. See how many shades you can come up with.

Paint effects

Different brush strokes can give you very different effects. Experiment to find which you enjoy using, and which brushes are best for different types of painting.

Look at the way the artist has painted these animals and see how many different effects you can get using different brush strokes, colours and materials.

This cat was painted quickly and in a loose style so that the colours blended together while still wet – it looks very effective from a distance.

The tip of a thin brush was used to paint the fine feathers on this toucan.

When painting this parrot, the artist first coloured it in watery paint. The details – beak, feathers and eyes – were added using drier paint and thin brushes.

Highlights

White highlights make these glasses and balloons look shiny. You can get this effect by leaving that part of the picture white (without paint), or by adding a few strokes of white paint when it is dry.

Different textures

You don't have to paint in solid colour. You can use thin brushes to do lots of different-coloured dots, or square-ended brushes to make lines of colour.

Try using a dry, stubby brush and dab nearly dry paint over different areas of your picture to make interesting textures, such as on this gingerbread man.

TIP

Keep experimenting with different paint effects to use in your pictures. You could try using a dry brush with nearly dry paint to make interesting textures.

No-brush art

You don't need a brush to paint! What about using sponges, rags, scraps of paper and fabric, or bits and pieces from around the house? You can even use your hands and fingers.

Home-made brushes

It's easy to make your own would–be 'brushes'. Try the examples shown below, or make up your own. What do the effects make you think of? How could you use them in your paintings?

TIP

Try different effects on scrap paper. Label your results so that you can remember how you did them. Experiment with different paints and different materials. Use your fingers and hands too!

Cotton wool makes puffs of steam or clouds.

Drag a twig through wet paint for a rough grass effect.

A sponge is good for making grass or soft animal fur.

Scrunched-up kitchen towel makes great textures.

Dragging paint

You can drag combs, plastic knives and forks, or the edge of a piece of cardboard through the paint to make patterns and markings.

Fingertip rabbit

1 Lightly draw the outline of the rabbit in pencil.

2 Now fill in the outline with different paints, using your fingers. Let each colour dry before adding the next one.

The grass in this picture was made with a mixture of thumb prints and a twig.

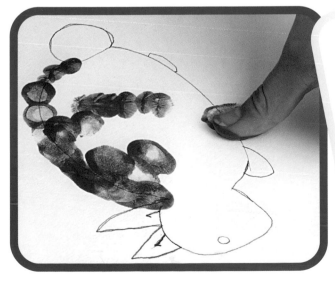

From a distance

Ever since the first artist picked up a brush, people have tried to paint the natural world around them. Here is a great project that will help you capture lots of different views in your paintings.

Paint a 3-D theatre

This **3-D** theatre is made up of cards, one placed behind the other, to make the scenery look realistic. Just as in a painting, you should make the front scenery strong using bold colours and the faraway parts paler.

WHAT YOU NEED
- Thin card
- Ruler and pencils
- Scissors
- Crayons and paint

3 Glue the concertina sides on to a card base. Cut out five rectangles of card, each 18 x 23cm. Paint one blue for the sky. Glue it to the sides to make the **backdrop**. Cut another rectangle into a frame shape and glue it to the front.

1 Cut two squares of thin card, each 18 x 18cm. Use a ruler to divide each square into ten 1.8cm lines

2 Fold along the lines to make two **concertina** shapes for the sides of your theatre.

2

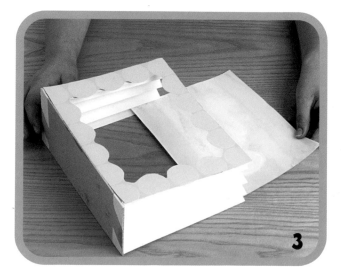

3

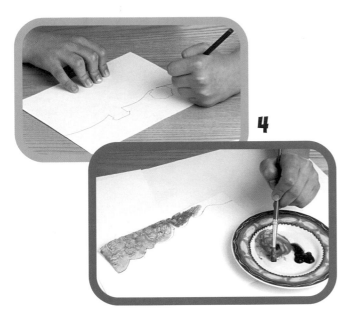

4 The three remaining rectangles are for your scenery. On one, use a pencil softly to sketch out a country scene with a house at the top. The other two pieces could include different-shaped hills with a fence or hedge. Draw these so that they are not as tall as the house scenery. The smaller scenes will slot in the front.

5 Now paint the scenery. Remember to use soft, pale colours in the distance, and strong, sharp details at the front. Finally, cut the pieces out, ready to slot into place in your 3-D theatre.

Create different sets of scenery for your theatre. What about a city at night?

6 Slot the cards into the theatre in the right order. This will show you how you can create a sense of distance in your paintings.

Painting with dots

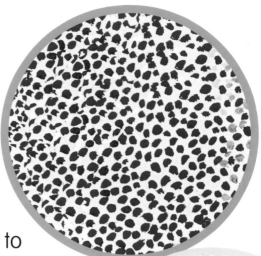

Do you know that there is a way to 'mix' colours so that you don't have to blend the paint on a **palette**? Put dots of different colours next to one another, and when you stand back, the colours appear to blend together!

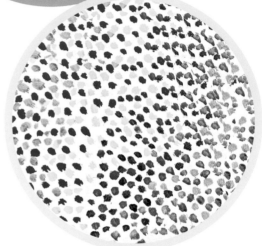

Dots and dashes

Practise using dots and dashes of colour before you begin painting.

1 Start making strokes with your first colour, leaving spaces between the strokes.

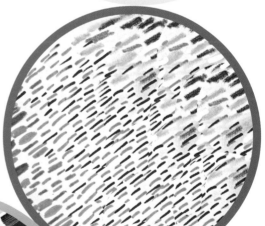

2 When the first colour is dry, fill in the spaces with strokes of a second colour. Now stand back from the image and look at it from a distance – what effect have you achieved? What happens if you add more dots?

These are some of the effects you can get using different colours and different size brushes and brush strokes.

Make a colourful dot painting

1 Use a soft pencil to sketch this picture onto paper.

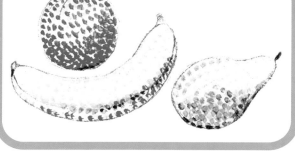

2 Colour each piece of fruit with dots of colour. Use one colour for each piece at first. Make the apple red, the banana yellow and the pear green.

3 Now create **shade** and highlights by adding dots of a darker colour. You can also create shade by adding more dots of the first colour.

4 When the fruit is complete, add a background in a warm, gentle colour.

17

Abstract art

You don't have to make your paintings look realistic if you don't want to. Many famous artists painted what they saw using flat patterns, bright colours and interesting shapes. This is called **abstract** art.

Different styles

Many artists moved away from realistic painting and developed styles of their own. **Pablo Picasso** often used a style called **cubism**, where everything is made of squares. **Henri Matisse** made images with blocks of colour.

**L'Escargot (The Snail)
by Henri Matisse**

TIP

Henri Matisse often used torn and cut paper to make bold **collages**.
Try making a collage of your artwork, using pieces of coloured paper instead of paint.

Make an abstract painting

Decide what you are going to paint – for example, the view from your window, a scene from a postcard, someone you know or an animal.

1 Lightly sketch the main parts of the picture with a pencil. Draw the houses and trees as simple shapes. In this painting, the artist hasn't tried to put anything in the right place – he has used the houses and trees to make a pattern of shapes and colours.

2 Paint the finished picture, using bold colours. Apply the paint in bold blocks of colour, without **shading**.

Painting patterns

Flowers, berries and leaves make great patterns. Look for examples in your garden, or when you go for a walk. Look through magazines, wallpaper and fabric samples to see how artists use natural forms in their designs. You can also make your own natural patterns.

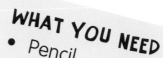
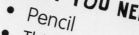

WHAT YOU NEED
- Pencil
- Thick paper
- Poster paints
- Scissors
- Glue

Design your own wallpaper or material

1 Look through your collection of leaves, flowers and plants. Sketch some of your favourite shapes, then cut them out.

2 Arrange the shapes in a pattern on a new sheet of paper, then glue them in the new arrangement.

3 For a repeat design, draw a grid with a pencil and ruler. This will help you to keep the shapes straight, the same size and in the right place. Your shapes can be realistic or imaginative.

4 Paint the pattern using poster paint. Which works best – two or three colours, or more? (Look at the tips on using colour on page 8–9.) Try matching colours together on a separate sheet of paper before making your final choice.

TIP

Victorian artists were keen on using nature in their designs. **William Morris** used plants, flowers and birds in wallpaper, **tapestries**, stained-glass windows, tiles and embroidery.

Dragging and combing

WHAT YOU NEED
- Very thick paint
- A wide brush
- Thick paper
- Pieces of stiff card or plastic packaging
- Scissors
- Glue

Dragging and combing pictures and designs in thick, wet paint is a fun way to create images.

1 Cut different comb shapes out of card. Make some of the combs with thick teeth, and some with thin teeth.

2 Divide your paper into roughly equal sections. Brush thick coats of paint in different colours on the separate sections.

3 While the paint is still wet, drag your card combs through the paint to make waves and lines. The colours will carry over into the other bands, and the paper will show through.

22

Scraper art

As well as making patterns, you can use your comb scrapers to make a picture.

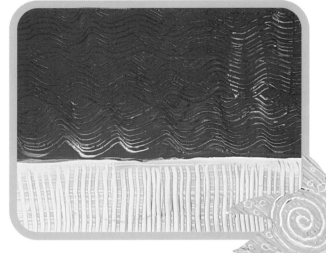

1 Paint a wide band of yellow across the bottom of the paper and fill in the rest of the page with blue paint. While the paint is still wet, use a comb to make swirly waves in the sea. Use a comb to make **horizontal** lines across the sand, then drag the comb upwards to give a **checked** effect.

2 On a separate piece of paper, use paint and combs to make sea animals and plants.

3 When these are dry, cut them out and glue them to the sea and sand background.

Can you think of any other swirly pictures to make? What else could you use to make marks in the paint?

23

Watery painting

You can get some wonderful effects if you brush watery paint onto wet paper. The colours blend together, giving a very soft result – perfect for painting skies and seas.

WHAT YOU NEED
- Watercolour paint
- Soft wide brush
- Thick paper
- Water in jar

Two-colour painting

Practise using two colours to make watery paintings.

1 Use a wide, soft brush to wet the paper. Then paint a wide strip of yellow across the bottom part of the paper.

2 Before it dries, dip your brush in the second colour. Brush this gently over the top so that the two colours merge softly. Work quickly before the paint dries!

TIP

If you don't want your paintings to crinkle when they dry, stretch the paper first. Dip the paper very quickly in water, and tape it to a piece of smooth wood or thick card using special gummed tape (from art shops). Once dry, it is ready to use.

Paint a sunset

1 Brush water all over the paper with a wide, soft brush. Paint the background in yellow. While the paint is wet, add some bold orange streaks.

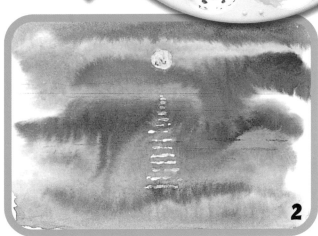

2 Now use some dark blue paint to add a band at the top of the image. Let this dry, then use white paint to add the sun and its reflection in the water.

3 Use black paint to make a strip of land about three-quarters of the way up the picture. Add some ripples in light blue in the foreground.

4 When the paint is dry, use a small brush and dry black paint to add the boats. They appear as **silhouettes** in the sunset, with dark reflections in the water.

Spatter art

Some artists don't use their brushes to paint objects, they just splatter the paint onto their pictures! It is a great way of making a fun, lively image with lots of colour.

Make your own messy masterpiece

1 Cover the floor with newspaper and wear an apron. Put your sheet of paper in the middle of the floor.

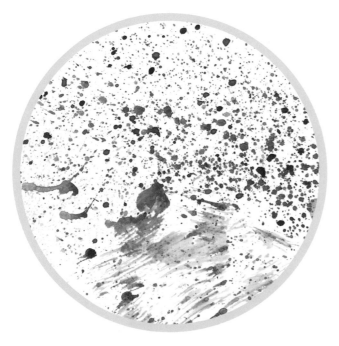

2 Flick runny paint onto the paper with brushes. Dip the toothbrush into paint, then point it at the paper and run the card over the bristles.

3 Add blobs, drizzles and splats of different colour, until you like the result. Leave some white background showing through.

Spatter stencils

You can create some really original pictures using this method.

1 Cut some shapes out of card, realistic ones or fantasy ones. Arrange them on a piece of paper.

2 Spatter the paint over the paper as before. Carefully lift up the shapes when you have finished.

TIP

If you want to make one or more areas of your picture darker, dip a toothbrush in paint then hold it near the area you want to make darker and keep flicking the paint at the paper using your thumb.

Going BIG!

Choose strong, simple images for a large painting or mural. The trick is to plan them first of all on a sheet of A4 paper. Then it's easy to scale them up in size.

What you need
- A4 paper
- A large piece of paper
- Ruler • Pencil
- Paint • Brushes

Using a graph to scale up

1 Sketch out your drawing or design on a small piece of paper. Paint in the colours you want to use.

2 When the paint has dried, draw a grid over the painting. Use a ruler and pencil to divide the picture into 5cm squares along the top and one side. Join the marks to make 5cm squares all over. If the picture doesn't divide exactly into 5cm squares, make the bottom rows slightly smaller.

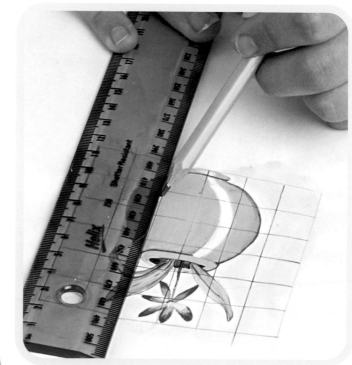

3 Now take your large piece of paper, and divide it into a grid with the same number of squares – but this time make the squares much bigger. Copy your picture, square by square, in pencil. When you are happy with it, paint it. Use your small painting as a guide to get the colours right.

TIP

If you don't want to spoil your first painting, tape a piece of tracing paper over the top, and draw the grid on this.

TIP

You can use this technique to create really huge pictures. Lots of different cultures make large images to decorate the walls of their houses or streets. Try making a large image for your classroom wall.

Glossary

3-D stands for three-dimensional – when an object has or appears to have height, width and depth

abstract pictures that do not look like real objects

backdrop the scenery in a theatre at the back of the stage

checked a pattern that's made up of squares

collage making pictures or patterns using different materials, such as paper and cloth, which are glued onto a background

complementary colours colours that work well together, like red and blue

concertina folding a piece of paper or card into small folds lengthways so that it has a shape like a fan

cubism a form of art in which pictures were made up of fragments of images

horizontal line or pattern running across the page, rather than up and down (which is called vertical)

Matisse, Henri French artist (1869–1954)

William Morris British artist and writer (1834–1896)

palettes specially made, flat pieces of wood or plastic which artists use to mix their paints on

Picasso, Pablo Spanish artist (1881–1973)

primary colours red, green and blue – the colours that mix to make all others

secondary colours the colours made by mixing the primary colours together

shade to add dark areas to a picture

silhouettes when objects are seen against a strong light they appear as dark shapes called silhouettes

sketchbook a book for making quick sketches to make into paintings later

tapestries a heavy fabric picture or design made by weaving coloured threads through it

Victorian the period of history when Queen Victoria was the monarch (1837–1901)

Index

Notes for teachers

The projects in this book are aimed at children at Key Stage 2. They can be used as stand-alone lessons or as a part of other areas of study.

While the ideas in the book are offered as inspiration, children should always be encouraged to paint from their own imagination and first-hand observations.

Sourcing ideas

All art projects should tap into children's interests, and be directly relevant to their lives and experiences. Try using stimulating starting points such as found objects, discussions about their family and pets, hobbies, TV programmes or favourite places.

Encourage children to source their own ideas and references, from books, magazines, the Internet or CD-ROM collections

Digital cameras can be used both to create reference material (pictures of landscapes, people or animals) and also used in tandem with children's finished work (see below).

Other lessons can often be an ideal springboard for an art project – for example, a geography field trip can be used as a source of ideas for a landscape picture.

Encourage children to keep a sketchbook to sketch ideas for future paintings, and to collect other images and objects to help them develop their work.

Give pupils as many first-hand experiences as possible through visits and contact with creative people.

Evaluating work

Arrange for the children to share their work with others, and to compare ideas and methods – this is often very motivating. Encourage them to talk about their work.

Show the children examples of other artists' paintings – how did they tackle the same subject and problems?

Help children to judge the originality and value of their paintings, to appreciate the different qualities in others' work and to value ways of working that are different from their own.

Going further

Look at ways of developing the projects further – for example, adapting the work into collage, print making or ceramics.

Use image-enhancing computer software and digital scanners to enhance, build up and juxtapose images.

Show the children how to develop a class art gallery on the school website.